Good Business

Ethics at Work

Second Edition

Advices and queries on personal standards of conduct at work

Contents

Published by

Quakers and Business Group   www.qandb.org

c/o Friends House

173-177 Euston Road

London NW1 2BJ

United Kingdom

ISBN 978-178456-068-3

Printed by www.printondemand-worldwide.com

Acknowledgements

The principal authors are members of the Quakers and Business Group, but we would like to acknowledge the many contributions and support which have come from the conference on Business and Ethics run by the Woodbrooke Quaker Study Centre, Birmingham, UK, in June 2000, and many other people in the UK and USA.

Introduction

Since the 18th century, businesses owned and run by Quakers have earned a reputation for trust, integrity, fair trading, care of their employees and betterment of the local community and society at large. Many of these businesses were hugely successful and, while no longer under the control of their founders' families, remain household names.

While working conditions are much better than in the 18th and 19th centuries, the world of work and business is still an imperfect one.

Today, many people are so dismayed by the unethical business practices they see around them that they believe that business itself is unethical. Some consider that making a profit is wrong. Those in business – ourselves included - know that to be sustainable a business must be profitable. But we also know that *what a business does* to make a profit affects individuals, communities and the environment - for good or bad.

The purpose of this book is to act as a guide and inspiration to running a better and ethical business for the benefit of *all* its stakeholders.

Quakers use a booklet entitled *Advices and Queries* as a challenge and inspiration in their personal lives. This book uses the same format. The advices and queries offered are not rules or requirements; rather they represent ideals to aspire to and standards of excellence to guide us.

Living up to these standards is not always the easiest course, but they have a practical as well as an ethical benefit. Businesses known for their ethical conduct enjoy benefits from a good reputation, customer loyalty and a more committed workforce.

You are invited to use these advices and queries alongside our methods for decision making to challenge and inspire your work and business.

List of Subjects

Quaker Testimonies
1. Honesty and integrity
2. Simplicity
3. Equality
4. Peace

Conduct of Business
5. Business and profit
6. Uncertainty and risk
7. Responsibilities of directors and managers
8. Obligations to shareholders and investors
9. Ethical trade
10. Environmental responsibility
11. Health, safety and security
12. Quality and safety of products and service
13. Advertising and promotion

Money Matters
14. Investments
15. Prompt payment
16. Financial accounts
17. Taxes
18. Remuneration
19. Gifts and donations

Working with People
20. Responsibility of employers to employees
21. Responsibility of employees to employers
22. Customers
23. Suppliers

Quaker Methods for Decision Making

The Quaker method of conducting meetings for business and arriving at decisions is quite different from that of most businesses.

The primary objective is to seek unity in decisions: to find a way forward that is acceptable to all present. This is not so easy to do, especially when the issue is a controversial one, or when there are strongly held opposing views. The outcome is not necessarily one that everyone agrees with, but one that all present can accept, in the knowledge that their views have been heard and considered. We must recognise that a minority view may continue to exist.

There are some Quaker ways of conducting meetings which others might find useful.

The use of silence

Silence itself has no magic. It may be just sheer emptiness or absence of sound. However, the effective use of silence in business meetings can create a powerful atmosphere for the receipt of inspiration and guidance.

Quaker meetings for business always begin and end with a period of silence. At the beginning the silence makes a break with the ego and what has gone before. It also gives time to focus on the task at hand and to concentrate on playing your part in discerning the way forward. Silence at the end helps to provide a peaceful closure and reflection.

Some of us have found that in tense or emotionally charged situations, a short period of silence can have a calming effect. When discussions become heated, the call for a few minutes' silence to reflect on the matter under consideration often helps.

Conduct of business meetings

Every meeting for business is chaired by an appointed clerk. The clerk's job is not just to keep the meeting going according to the agenda, or to record the proceedings in minutes that will be disseminated afterwards. The clerk's primary role is to be able to gauge the sense of the meeting, and to bring minds together so that an acceptable way forward can be agreed. When the way forward has been found, the clerk drafts a minute recording the decision, which is agreed by all those present.

This method takes patience and insight, but it has advantages. It enables all opinions to be heard so that everyone should be comfortable with the outcome. It creates clarity because the minute has been agreed at the time, whilst the issues are fresh in people's minds. This reduces subsequent differences of opinion and revisions to minutes. The entire meeting has ownership of the minutes.

Meeting for clearness

This is a special form of meeting to help a person or group of people make a difficult decision or to seek guidance at times of change or difficulty. A small number of people are appointed for their special knowledge or experience to help those present become clear about possible options and ways forward. A relaxed atmosphere of trust is important and confidentiality must be maintained within the group. A facilitator should be chosen to assist in clarifying the questions. This is a time for listening with undivided attention.

Quaker Testimonies

Quakers live in accordance with four core principles, or testimonies: Honesty and integrity, Simplicity, Equality and Peace. These testimonies are not imposed, but guide their personal and professional lives.

1. Honesty and integrity

Advice   The most important word to remember in all business dealings is 'integrity'. Integrity is essential to developing trust: People act with integrity when they are not moved by opportunist or self-seeking impulses and their response to a total situation can be trusted. Integrity involves being open, honest, truthful and consistent with your beliefs and values in all business dealings.

The whole of business requires trust, faith and goodwill. Establishing trust is a critical success factor.

Queries   Are you honest and truthful in all you say and do? If under pressure do you lower your standard of integrity? Do you resist pressure?

Do you do what you promise, even if it is just to return a phone call?

2. Simplicity

Advice
The most serene and happy people are often those who live a simple life. By contrast, stress, overwork and insecurity are rife in today's pressured world of business. In business, as in our personal life, we can be consumed by our own desires for more, as well as by the demands of others. The practice of simplicity helps us to eliminate the superfluous and to put first things first. This requires strong principles, focused vision, deep understanding, clear communication and deliberate action.

Queries
Do you make time to review your priorities? When faced with conflicting demands, do you look at them in the light of your priorities and endeavour to put the more important things first?

Do you scrutinise your desires and consider how you might simplify your needs? Are you easily persuaded to buy something you do not need or cannot afford? Is there a need for lavish entertainment or expensive offices? Can you achieve the same objective in a different way?

Can you simplify your processes and procedures and still accomplish your business purpose?

3. Equality

Advice   All people are of equal worth and deserve to be treated as such. Discrimination is divisive. Be alert to practices here and throughout the world that discriminate against people on the basis of who or what they are or because of their beliefs.

Queries   Do you respect and encourage diversity as a source of energy in your business?

Do you refrain from making prejudiced judgements about others?

When recruiting, evaluating or promoting employees, do you differentiate on the grounds of age, gender, sexual orientation, skin colour, religion, nationality or dialect, or any other characteristic that is not related to job performance?

If an employee has a disability, do you try to find work that they can do effectively? Do you make alterations in your working methods and workplace to help them? Do you help them to overcome their own difficulties?

4. Peace

Conflict happens, and will continue to happen, even in the most peaceful of worlds. In business, as in the rest of life, how we deal with our own anger and how we find peaceful solutions to conflict are important. What matters most, however, is to work towards creating a culture of peace overcoming the potential for all war and strife. This requires searching out anything in our conduct of business which might contain the seeds of war or otherwise threaten life.

Quakers believe that there is good in everyone. This leads to one of their most strongly held beliefs that it is wrong to kill anyone and therefore all forms of war are wrong. Conflict should be pre-empted through active peace-keeping and, when it does flare up, should be resolved while preserving respect for all concerned.

Avoid doing any business which promotes warfare in any form.

When you disagree with a colleague, customer or supplier, are you willing to consider that you may be mistaken? Do you give others the benefit of the doubt?

When you are angry, do you act in a destructive manner, or are you able to express your anger in a way that allows a solution to be found?

What is your fundamental attitude towards business? Do you believe that success is achieved primarily by overcoming the competition at any cost?

Does your company earn any income from practices which threaten human life?

Conduct of Business

We are all stewards accountable for our use of time, people, money and natural resources. A good steward seeks the right balance between prudence and adventure; conservatism and creation; leading and serving; stimulating and supporting.

Good business is the way we serve the social and economic community, whether individually or corporately in national or international organisations. Its principles apply equally to commercial enterprises, charities and not-for-profit enterprises, as all are managed by individuals aiming to optimise performance.

5. Business and profit

Advice   There is nothing unethical in making a profit. No business will survive for long without it. What matters is how you make your profit and what you do with it.

If you want to maintain, or even increase, employment, it will be necessary to be profitable and to build up resources for the future. Profit is also needed for new development and to contribute to the community in which you operate.

Queries   Are the purposes of your business clear to all your stakeholders? Are all its activities focused on achieving its objectives?

What is the driving force of your business? Is it just to maximise your profit or is it to provide sustainable employment for as many people as is sensible; to build your employees' confidence, skills and sense of worth; to provide a product or service that contributes to others' well-being? Does it allow for your business to have a sustainable future?

Is your profit gained in an ethical and just way? If you have little competition, do you make an excessive profit? In the conduct of your business, do you provide good quality at a fair and fixed price? Are you tempted to raise your prices and make a bigger profit just because the market will bear it?

6. Uncertainty and risk

Advice

There is an element of uncertainty and risk in every business. There can be uncertainty because we lack information about the situation, the future or the consequences of an action. There is always the risk of loss either from a particular course of action or from an unexpected occurrence.

It is important to be proactive in managing and containing risks so as not to risk the livelihood of your employees or the future survival of your business.

Do you regularly review the risks associated with your business and seek competent advice on how to manage them?

Do you take reasonable steps to remove unnecessary risks? Do you make sure that people affected by a risk know about it? Do you seek to contain and limit the consequences through appropriate insurance? Do you have contingency plans ready to deal with unexpected events?

Do you take unnecessary risks, potentially damaging the livelihood of your employees or the future of your business?

7. Responsibilities of directors and managers

Directors and managers are responsible to all stakeholders of the business. These include investors, government bodies and the community, as well as employees, customers and suppliers.

A business should fully comply with all applicable laws and regulations. If you consider a law to be at variance with your own social or ethical values, seek advice before taking action.

Seek to do away with dangers and abuses by creating an atmosphere and culture in your workplace that encourages health, safety, integrity and well-being as well as high productivity.

Are you aware of your legal responsibilities as a director or manager? Do you fulfil them?

Do you regularly review the social and moral health of your business? Do you set, communicate and work to standards of business conduct? Have you established systems for monitoring and reporting back in these areas?

If your organisation is doing something which you believe to be unethical, do you consider what part you must play to put the matter right?

Do you ensure that your shareholders receive all the information they need to rightly value and appraise their investment?

8. Obligation to shareholders and investors

Advice Any sizeable company needs outside investors in order to take advantage of opportunities for growth. Shareholders provide necessary capital and are rewarded by dividends or capital growth.

Small shareholders have a small voice in the running of a company, but their concerns should be listened to and considered, or your reputation as a business may suffer.

Queries Do you ensure that your shareholders receive a fair return for their investment and risk? Are you managing for the long-term security of their investment?

Do you avoid necessary expenditure in order to increase the return to your shareholders?

Do your communications with your shareholders give sufficient information about the progress of the company?

9. Ethical trade

Advice   Wages should reflect the contribution workers make to their companies. Wages and work requirements should enable them to meet their own needs and those of their dependants, and to contribute to the sustainable growth of their community. Paying below a living wage could be regarded as a form of modern slavery.

Queries   Does your company invest in, or have offices in, or buy from, countries where there are on-going violations of human rights?

Does your company contract with companies which employ children under the age of 15, who are prevented from obtaining a basic education because of their work?

Does your company contract with companies which do not pay their employees a sustainable living wage in their own community?

10. Environmental responsibility

Advice   We have a responsibility to care for the physical and economic environment of the whole world. We should consider the effect our business has beyond our immediate environment and see the wider environment as a 'silent stakeholder'.

Consider your immediate environment and ensure you do not cause a nuisance to neighbours - by excessive noise, the production of noxious fumes, or keeping your premises untidy.

Queries   Do you consider the way your goods or services contribute to a sustainable world environment? Do you have an active pollution prevention programme? Do you search for ways to reduce and eliminate waste? Do you upcycle, recycle or use recyclable parts?

Do you provide a product or service which is in any way harmful to life? If so, are there clear warnings?

Do you have an environmental policy and report annually on your progress?

11. Health, safety and security

Advice All employers and employees have a duty to ensure that their working practices and equipment are safe for all users and the general public. They should also exercise caution and take steps to minimise risks to the health, safety and welfare of others, whether they are employees, customers or anyone affected by the products or services supplied.

Queries Do you take all reasonable and appropriate steps to comply with health and safety regulations? Do you compromise on safety measures to save money?

Do you work with others to ensure that best practices, standards, regulations and legislation are developed to promote public well-being?

When you see something which could be a hazard, do you report it?

12. Quality and safety of products and services

Advice Quakers have a long-standing reputation for providing good quality at a fair price. This reputation enhanced their businesses. There is plenty of evidence to show that this is good practice for any business and pays its own dividends.

Suppliers have a responsibility to ensure that what they offer does not cause foreseeable physical or financial damage to their users.

Queries   Do you continually strive to improve the quality and safety of your products? Do you have a quality control programme?

Does your product have a built-in obsolescence, so that the customer will have to replace it soon?

Do your products and services comply with the law and other regulations? Are they safe, fit for use, suitable for their purpose, appropriately designed and sustainably produced?

Have your products been carefully assessed for possible damage or loss they could cause to customers? Have you provided adequate warnings of any dangers? Have you ensured others can be compensated in the event that your product causes unforeseen harm or dissatisfaction?

13. Advertising and promotion

Advice   Advertising and promotional activities are a real test of our commitment to honesty and integrity in business. Consider carefully your reasons for advertising, what your advertisements say (or omit to say), and where you advertise.

Queries   Are you careful to avoid intentionally misleading
those with whom you do business? Do you ensure
that your claims and promises are justified and
realistic?

Do your promotions present a true and accurate
picture of your products and services?

Are you selling goods and services of worth or are
you selling image? Are you aiming your
advertisements at particularly vulnerable markets,
such as children?

Is your advertising right use of resources? Are the
costs of promotion an appropriate proportion of
the overall price?

Money Matters

Money is a complex commodity. Our use of money has the power to do great good or great evil. It should be remembered that money has extremely powerful, symbolic and psychological connotations and implications that can lead people to behave unexpectedly. In business, money should be used like any other tool – to help achieve your business objectives. An excess of money should not become a goal in itself.

14. Investments

Advice   Think carefully how you invest any surplus funds not immediately needed. Whilst these funds are being invested, someone else is making use of them. Is that use something you would approve of?

Seek to invest in activities or enterprises that contribute positively to the local or global economy, and which raise the quality and standard of living.

Consider the conditions under which the income is produced and the effect which the investment may have on the welfare of all.

Queries   Does your company invest in, or earn revenue from, activities that are unethical or harmful to life? These may include alcohol, drugs, tobacco, firearms or military weapons and supplies, or gambling.

When you have surplus funds, do you keep some back for when your business will need them?

Do you look after your reserve funds properly, or could they be used more effectively? Do you consider ethical investments, even if the return might be slightly less?

Do you use money entrusted to you with prudence, discretion and responsibility?

If you lend money, is the loan properly recorded? Do you charge a higher rate of interest than you could earn on the money if you invested it elsewhere?

15. Prompt payment

Advice

Remember that payment is owed when the job is completed. Many small businesses may experience serious cash flow problems and even become bankrupt because they do not have sufficient cash to pay their own bills. Often this is because other companies – larger or with more trading influence – have not paid them on a timely basis, not because they are unprofitably managed. Make sure you pay your bills on time.

Queries   Do you know and honour your suppliers' terms? Do you delay payment at the expense of your supplier?

Do you make your own terms clear and do you deal fairly and consistently with those who do not honour them?

16. Financial accounts

Advice   Accounts are important statements about your business. They should accurately reflect your business position. The information they contain should be appropriately available to those who trade with you so that they can assess any risk.

Unless you keep careful accounts and review them each month it is difficult to manage the business properly. Do not rely solely on historic figures. It is important to consider the future and to try to forecast likely events.

Ensure that people handling money are competent, that they are honest and that they are not presented with undue temptation.

Queries   Do you ensure that you keep true and accurate accounts? Are your annual accounts produced in a timely manner?

Do you audit your accounting systems to ensure that the control mechanisms are adequate? Are you vigilant against fraud, honest mistakes and intended deceit?

Do you provide your accounts to those who need to know about your business for their well-being, including your staff?

17. Taxes

Advice Good organisation of your financial affairs in order to pay not more than the tax you legally owe is good management. Evading tax by arranging your affairs in order to escape paying taxes which are properly due is theft. It is important to consider carefully the line separating the two. Not all professional advisers are clear on the distinction.

Queries When a way of avoiding tax is suggested, do you consider carefully whether this is avoidance and not evasion? Do you allow these opportunities to influence the organisation of your business' finances?

Do you deal honestly with the tax authorities? Do you consider paying tax as part of the duty of your business to society?

Do you keep careful records to prevent evasion of tax, National Insurance and VAT?

Do you keep adequate records of benefits in kind so that Her Majesty's Revenue and Customs is not defrauded or your staff penalised?

Do you take steps to ensure that cash transactions are accurately reported for tax purposes?

18. Remuneration

Advice

Remuneration is not just about pay. It may also include bonuses, company pension contributions, privileged share purchases and services (including cars) provided by the company. It is a return for work done, responsibility and good management.

Rates of remuneration are subject to market forces. Be aware that excessive remuneration can cause envy, which is dangerous to a free society.

Any differences in pay between people doing similar jobs should be logical and understood by all concerned.

Queries

If you award yourself high remuneration, does the same principle apply throughout the company? Do you have a fixed ratio within the company comparing the highest to the lowest paid?

Is your remuneration linked to performance and profitability, even when this has been achieved by making others redundant?

Good Business: Ethics at Work

Do you ensure that your wages and salaries are adequate so that employees do not depend on benefits or other means to supplement their pay? Do you pay only the least salary and other benefits you can get away with?

Do you ensure that part-time staff receive the same benefits as full-time staff, on a proportionate scale?

Do you provide a pension for your employees? Is it fully portable (including your contributions) when the employee leaves your employment?

If your staff have to work overtime, do you give them fair recompense?

If staff live in accommodation which is tied to the job, is provision being made by either the employer or yourself for their accommodation after they retire?

Do you have a profit sharing plan, to which all (including part-time employees) belong?

19. Gifts and donations

Advice

Encourage a spirit of generosity in your company. Set aside a portion of your profit for charitable purposes. Consider providing an amount of company time for employees to use in support of a worthy cause.

Sometimes gifts can be acceptable as a sign of appreciation, but be careful that this is not seen as a bribe. If you donate to political parties or pressure groups, be open about it in your accounts.

Queries

Do you set aside some money for charitable purposes each year? Do you give your employees the opportunity to decide how some of this should be allocated?

Do you encourage your staff to give to charities personally and do you provide procedures and mechanisms for helping them to do so?

If you give gifts - without expectation of favours in return - are you sure that the receiver is not taking on an obligation?

If a business colleague invites you out, do you pay on at least half of the occasions?

Do you have a policy on accepting gifts?

Good Business: Ethics at Work

Working with People

Consider that in your professional life you are engaged, with others, in a journey of development – practically, intellectually, emotionally and spiritually.

Treat other people in the way in which you would like to be treated. Remember that people have different values and that you might be dealing with people from a culture that is different from yours. Like ourselves, at different times people might be angry, hurt or distracted and they might make mistakes or do things that are hurtful.

20. Responsibility of employers to employees

Advice   During the early twentieth century, Quakers pioneered better ways of treating people at work that are now accepted as normal practice. Quaker businesses took a leading part in reducing working hours, providing sick benefit, pensions, life assurance and, in some cases, affordable housing.

One of the primary responsibilities of business today is the creation of opportunity for people of all ages. Employers have a responsibility to bring out the best in people and encourage their moral and intellectual growth. They should seize opportunities to improve the well-being of their employees.

If or when disputes occur, it is easier to deal with tensions and perhaps take difficult action early on than it is to try to resolve conflicts and make peace after a difficulty has developed into a destructive, full-scale dispute. A clear dispute or grievance procedure that is known and accepted by all can take the heat out of a disagreement and allow a speedy and just resolution.

Queries   Are people proud to work for your company? Do your employees consider your business a good place to work?

Are your places of work safe, healthy, cheerful and pleasant?

Do you treat your employees in the same way that you would like to be treated?

Do you give volunteers the same care, consideration and recognition as employees?

Are your working hours flexible enough to allow for family commitments?

Do you provide adequate training for your employees so that they can progress either in your business or another when an opportunity arises?

Do you support your staff when they decide to leave? Do you provide fair references? When you have to dismiss an employee, for whatever reason, do you do it as kindly as possible? In a case of redundancy, do you compensate your employee for (some of) the time it will take them to find another job?

Do you have a regular programme of performance reviews and do you adhere to it?

Do you seek to avoid and prevent unnecessary disputes? Do you have ways to detect disputes and deal with them before they become disruptive? Do you have a clear grievance procedure that emphasises mediation or arbitration?

21. Responsibility of employees to an employer

Advice   Your employer is providing you and possibly your family with a livelihood. You should recognise that in return you must earn your keep. Whatever your position, make sure that you take your share of the responsibility to make the company a success.

The workplace provides many facilities, opportunities and distractions. These might include chat, telephones, e-mail, photocopiers, internet access, and so on. Make sure these are used for the furtherance of the business. Use for private convenience, entertainment or gain should be kept to a minimum. Remember that to go beyond reasonable use is a betrayal of your employer's trust and is in fact theft.

Queries   Do you give a full day's work for your wage, salary or commission? Do you avoid wasting your employer's or client's time? Do you spend unnecessary time socialising on the job?

Do you speak up and tell your employer when there are problems or when you see difficulties ahead?

Do you ask for permission to use company facilities for your own purposes?

Do you treat your employer the way you would wish to be treated? Do you uphold the reputation of your company to others outside work?

Are you pleasant, courteous, helpful and supportive to customers, suppliers and other employees?

22. Customers

Advice   Treat your relationship with your customers with respect. Try to base your transactions and exchanges on fairness and equality so neither party feels aggrieved or mistreated.

Conventional wisdom is that the customer is always right, but this must be accepted with care. Reserve the right to decline custom from someone who does not respect your own rights.

Be careful not to pass information learned from one customer on to another, especially when the two are in competition.

All businesses will receive complaints from customers. Sometimes they are fair, and sometimes they are not; but all complaints have to be dealt with if your reputation as a fair supplier is to be maintained.

Queries   Do you treat your customers with the respect they deserve?

If you are likely to work for two customers in the same industry, do you inform both customers and tell them what steps you take to preserve the confidence of each?

If you are going to be late in delivery, do you tell your customer as soon as possible, or do you wait until they complain? Do you do all you can to minimise the problem for your customer?

Is your invoice comparable with your quotation – or are there lots of extras?

Do you decline custom from someone who does not respect your rights?

Are you willing to listen to and learn from any complaints? Do you replace faulty goods without question? Do you have a fair complaints procedure? Do you take all reasonable steps to deal with complaints as quickly as possible and to rectify an error as soon as it is found?

23. Suppliers

Advice

Treat the relationship with your suppliers in the same spirit as your customer relationships. Suppliers have just as much right to be respected as customers. They are equally important to your business success. They may also be a customer one day.

Queries

Do you treat suppliers with the respect they deserve?

If you have a strong purchasing position, do you treat your suppliers harshly, abusing the power this gives you? If you want to end a long-standing relationship with a supplier, do you give enough notice for them to adjust their business?

When a supplier provides credit, they are lending you their money. Do you treat that privilege with the respect it deserves?

Do you strive to achieve lasting relationships of mutual trust with your suppliers? Do you keep them waiting for appointments?

Do you ask an unnecessary number of suppliers to provide quotations? Remember that every quotation takes time to prepare. Do you expect suppliers to provide free work when giving a quotation? Do you provide someone else's quotation as a target to beat?

Do you ask for quotations without intending to change suppliers, but only to reduce the charges of an existing supplier?

Do you ensure that you have contracts with your suppliers – for their protection as well as for yours? Do you give your suppliers prompt, clear and helpful feedback when their goods or services are not up to the standard expected?

24. Competitors

Advice

Respect your competitors. Remember that together you are looking after the reputation of your whole industry. Within the spirit and intent of the law, consider working jointly with your competitors to provide a new or better product or service. Avoid wasteful or hurtful associations, cartels and monopolies that damage the economy, the environment or other people.

Queries

Do you avoid maligning your competitors?

Do you desist from industrial espionage? If confidential information concerning a competitor is made available to you, do you refrain from making use of it? Do you take reasonable and prudent precautions to protect your business and its employees from industrial espionage, hackers and malicious attacks?

Are you willing to refer a customer to a competitor when you cannot provide their needs? Do you try to entice customers away from your competitors by unethical means?

Do you avoid price-fixing arrangements?

Good Business: Ethics at Work

25. Caring for oneself

Advice   Business, like other activities in life, requires that each person takes good care of themselves.

Develop personal habits, routines and rituals that limit the stress and pressure in your life. Build your own self-discipline to work and rest effectively, living a rich life of benefit to all.

Queries   Do you take sufficient rest and holidays to ensure you are effective in your job?

Do you ensure that you know both yourself and your business and that you set realistic and achievable objectives? Are you learning to face issues and situations so that you avoid unnecessary fear and poor decisions? Do you seek wise counsel from both inside and outside your business when in difficulties and when contemplating new directions?

Do you know when to let go, whether it be to others, to sell, or to retire?

Are you careful to share your burdens as well as your joys? Do you allow others to take a full part in the work and responsibility of your business so that neither you nor they are over-burdened or over-stressed? Do you praise and value yourself as well as your employees?

The Community

A business is involved in communities at many levels. First of all companies must build a thriving community within their organisation. At the next level a company is involved in the larger community, including suppliers, customers, governments and others. At the highest level companies, regardless of size, are involved in the global economy. The world of business demonstrates the interdependence of the whole human race.

26. Local community

Advice   The community in which you operate consists of residents, other businesses, schools, shops and other services. Although it is easier to be recognised for what you do in a small community, in a large city the same concern for the community applies.

Try to make your business an asset to the community and not an annoyance.

If asked to support a local activity, try to participate in some way.

Queries   Are you actively involved in working for the improvement of the community in which you work?
How does your reputation stand locally?

Are you vigilant against earning undue profit at the cost of the community?

27. Government

Advice   Business is required to operate within both the spirit and intent of the law: local, national and international. Monitoring and understanding the impact of legislation is difficult and time consuming. In most instances, laws do not affect businesses that manage their affairs ethically; however, ignorance of the law is no excuse. If you discover you are operating outside the law, correct the situation as quickly as possible.

Queries   In all your business affairs, do you keep within the law? Do you make sure that you are regularly informed about regulations that apply to your business? Do you respect and abide by them?

Do you join with others and take steps to change those laws and regulations which you believe are unjust or immoral?

28. Trade Unions

Advice   Remember that it is the job of trade unions to assert the interest of their members, particularly by pressing for security of employment, good working conditions and the most favourable rates of pay possible. In your dealings with trade unions, work to cultivate a mutual trust that delivers organisation success. The objective of negotiations is to achieve a beneficial outcome for both parties.

Queries   Do you keep any promises you may have made to trade unions? Do you ask more from them than you would be prepared to give if you were in their position?

Do you try to avoid unnecessary conflict and confrontation? Do you consider employers and trade unions as colleagues, each of whom has a worthwhile contribution to make to the business?

29. Pressure groups

Advice   Sometimes a product or service, a price, or a lack of competition can be seen by a vocal minority to be wrong. If you are affected, do not ignore the situation, but consider carefully what is said and what, if anything, you should do about it.

Queries   If your business is the subject of a pressure group, do you take time to talk to them, to understand their points of view, to explain yours, and to try and come to an amicable way of resolving problems?

Do you join with others to work for a better, more moral world? Do you ensure that any pressure groups to which you may belong are morally based?

Unethical Business Practices

Many people in business have at one time or another been confronted with unethical business practices. These practices have helped to give business a bad reputation. How we respond to these situations can involve having to make difficult decisions, even to the point of blowing the whistle and bringing the matter to the attention of an outside body.

30. Gambling and speculation

Advice   In gambling we gain by the outcome of some chance event and from the losses of other people. When we invest in exceptionally risky ventures with the hope of a large return in the future, we are speculating.

Unjustified confidence and optimism or an addiction to the excitement of uncertainty can lead to disaster. In a working environment this might put your employees' livelihood at stake.

Queries   Do you invest or use company funds for speculation or gambling?

Do you entertain business colleagues at casinos or other venues where gambling takes place?

31. Corrupt practices

Advice

Bribes, back-handers and other practices which we would consider corrupt are commonly accepted in some industries and cultures. Make sure that your employees know that these kinds of practices are not acceptable.

Queries

Do you have a clear written policy on business conduct which all employees sign?

Do you avoid all forms of bribery and corruption, both within your own business and in your dealings with business partners?

When you work in cultures where bribery and corruption are part of the way of life, do you try to find ways of doing business that more closely express your own ethical standards?

Do you discourage and work against sharp practice in all your workplaces? Do you speak out against the corrupt practices you discover?

32. Whistle blowing

Advice

Before blowing the whistle on an organisation, or on a particular business practice, consider carefully the consequences of your actions. Your role is to be a witness to the truth. Be sure that you understand the reasons for the practice and that your evidence is clear, complete and unambiguous. Make sure that your own motives will withstand public scrutiny.

Act promptly as soon as you are sure of what you intend to do. Where possible, seek advice and guidance from others. Work through an agency to remove undue emotions and personalities from the situation allowing truth and facts to prevail.

Queries   Is the action you contemplate likely to lead to a change for the better? If not, what is your motivation? Is there a better, less confrontational, way of dealing with the situation? Do you realise that your action might cost you your job and that will affect your personal life and your career? Have you sought independent, wise counsel before proceeding?

Is your company's culture one where your staff and colleagues have the confidence to deal with corruption? Do you have procedures in place so that your employees can, if necessary, blow the whistle without being penalised?

Balancing Vision with Practice

Visions, ideals, principles and aims are not enough. They need to be translated into action in our daily lives. The means are as important as the ends we seek to achieve.

None of us are perfect. Our methods and practices must take account of our own limitations and capacity for mistakes as well as the failures and frailties of others.

Balancing discipline, especially self-discipline, with freedom and exploration are perhaps the most important way that we develop and realise our business vision and goals.

33. Leadership and decision making

Advice   In each business situation someone needs to take the initiative to point the way forward and to motivate others to realise the common vision. We are all called upon to lead at different times.

In business situations it is important to share your views with others, and consider the best way to achieve them. Consider all the stakeholders affected, not just those most affected or closest. Planning to realise a vision is not sufficient – it is necessary to make a decision and to act.

Queries   Are you prepared to take responsibility for decision making? Do you consult with those affected first? Do you avoid paralysing indecision?

Are you open to the advice and guidance of colleagues?

When a decision has been made, do you explain it to those affected so that they understand the vision and the part which they have in its realisation? Are your decisions justified and will they withstand scrutiny?

34. Management

Advice

Good management is the skill of allocating resources, planning, and organising other people in the performance of their work. This means giving people a framework in which to work and enabling them to do a good job despite any limitations.

Good managers need to nurture a spirit of teamwork to get the best out of their people. Determine the elements that make your workplace a happy and effective one, and then create them.

Queries

Do you respect your employees? Do you trust everyone, even though in some cases this may be betrayed?

Do you set a positive example to others in the way you manage your business? Does your managerial competence and behaviour earn their respect? Do you avoid destructive cultures of blame, belittling and humiliation?

Do you communicate your plans, concerns and expectations clearly, appropriately and in a timely manner?

Do you delegate? Do you try to make each person's job more satisfying by giving them as much responsibility as they can manage?

If you supervise others, do you remember that this is your opportunity to help them to contribute their best? Do you give spontaneous feedback – both praise and correction? Are you careful to praise and reward others for their efforts and achievements? Do you pass on compliments from your customers? If someone makes a mistake do you consider how you can help the person concerned?

Do you remember that everyone has their own personal life and problems and may, from time to time, need your support?

When difficult situations arise, do you remember that even those who are hostile or who abuse our trust must be treated fairly and legally? Are you careful to keep an objective record of events?

35. Monitoring, awareness and audits

Advice   Every good business needs systems to monitor
what is happening, so that it can be alert to
problems when they emerge, and take action to
correct the situation quickly. Monitoring, auditing
and feed-back are important for quality control,
continuous improvement and performance
assessment.

These activities should take place in an open and
constructive way. Those people responsible for
monitoring should be appropriately qualified and
respect the rights of individuals.

Queries   Does your business have sufficient systems for
monitoring, auditing and assurance? Do you
ensure that the people engaged in monitoring are
suitable and qualified for their tasks?

Do you ensure that the results of your monitoring
and performance measurement are fed back to
people constructively and sensitively? Do you use
monitoring and feed-back to improve people's
quality of life at work as well as to improve the
business's performance?

36. Confidentiality

Advice   Anything that is personal to an individual,
including that person's feelings and even your
observations about them, is confidential. Treat
anything in a one-to-one meeting as confidential –

unless it is clearly for public consumption. Similarly, always treat discussions about an individual in confidence.

Be aware that in a business situation, under current human rights legislation, any employee might be entitled to know what has been written or even said about them in a meeting.

Comply with both the spirit and the intent of legislation designed to protect the privacy of others.

Queries   Can people confide in you with confidence? Do you use information entrusted to you with discretion and responsibility? Are you careful to respect the privacy of others?

Do you take care to ensure that no-one's rights, privacy or confidentiality are impaired or abused? Are you careful not to take ideas from one supplier and give them to another?

Are you careful not to use or distribute confidential information? If you receive confidential material belonging to a competitor - what do you do with it?

37. Intellectual property

Advice   Recognise that copyright initially belongs to the originator, but this might be assigned to an employer or sold to a third party. If you want to copy or use someone else's work, do not avoid paying for and acknowledging their ownership. In the same way, make sure that your company's intellectual property is legally protected.

Queries   Do you take prudent steps to ensure that you do not infringe the copyrights, patents, or other intellectual property rights of others? Do you acknowledge the sources of your work?

Before you make photocopies or use artwork do you check to find out who owns the copyright? Do you ask for permission to use the material? Do you make sure that the changes you make are acceptable to the owner? Are you careful about copies made for private study? Do you use computer software which you have not paid for?

Do you use all necessary legal means at your disposal to register and protect your own intellectual property?

If you, or your company, invent something which may, or ought to be, in the public domain, how do you decide what fee to charge for its use? Is it what the market will bear or what is right?

If you do not protect your rights, how do you prevent a less ethical supplier from usurping your copyright and charging highly for the product?

Useful Contacts

Business Ethics

Institute of Business Ethics
24 Greencoat Place
London SW1P 1BEJ
Tel: 020 7798 6040
www.ibe.org.uk

International Business
Ethics Institute
1776 I Street NW, 9th Floor
Washington DC 20006 USA
Tel: +1 202 296 6938
www.business-ethics.org

Business Management

The Work Foundation
21 Palmer Street
London, SW1H 0AD
Tel: 020 7976 3512
www.theworkfoundation.com

Investors in People
UKCES, Sanctuary Buildings
20 Great Smith Street
London SW1P 3BT
Tel: 0300 303 3033
www.investorsinpeople.co.uk

Co-Operatives UK
Holyoake House
Hanover Street
Manchester M60 0AS
www.uk.coop

Social Enterprise UK
The Fire Station
139 Tooley Street
London SE1 2HZ
Tel: 020 3589 4950
www.socialenterprise.org.uk

Ethical Investment Association
Holywell Centre
1 Phipp Street
London, EC2A 4PS
Tel: 020 7749 9950
www.ethicalinvestment.org.uk

Public Concern at Work (The Whistleblowing Charity)
3rd Floor, Bank Chambers
6 - 10 Borough High Street
London SE1 9QQ
Tel: 020 3117 2520
www.pcaw.org.uk

About the
Quakers and Business Group

The Quakers and Business Group (Q&B) was founded in 1998, registered as a charity in 2002, and as a Charitable Incorporated Organisation in 2014. The group is run using the Quaker Business Method described in this book.

The group's objective is 'to promote Quaker principles in business and the workplace'.

It works on a wide range of projects concerning ethical and responsible practices, carries out research, runs events, and supports those with a business need or concern.

It is open to all of any faith, or none, who have an interest in business and employment practices, from the private, public, social and charity sectors.

Q&B membership is international, with a LinkedIn Group. www.qandb.org

Quakers in the United Kingdom
(Religious Society of Friends)
Friends House
173-177 Euston Road
London NW1 2BJ
Tel: 020 7663 1000
www.quaker.org.uk